Arctic Animals

Snowy Owls

ABDO
Publishing Company

Big Buddy BOOKS
Arctic Animals

by Julie Murray

Published by ABDO Publishing Company, PO Box 398166, Minneapolis, Minnesota 55439.

Printed in the United States of America, North Mankato, Minnesota.
032013
012014

 PRINTED ON RECYCLED PAPER

Coordinating Series Editor: Rochelle Baltzer
Editor: Marcia Zappa
Contributing Editors: Megan M. Gunderson, Sarah Tieck
Graphic Design: Maria Hosley
Cover Photograph: *Shutterstock*: Andrzej Fryda.
Interior Photographs/Illustrations: *Getty Images*: Steven Kazlowski (p. 17), Winfried Wisniewski/Foto Natura (p. 27);
    Glow Images: Bruce J. Lichtenberger (p. 19), Wayne Lynch (pp. 17, 23), Winfried Schäfer (p. 8), Christine und
    J©rgen Sohns (p. 27), Egmont Strigl (p. 9), ARCO / Wiede, U. & M. (pp. 21, 25); *iStockphoto*: ©iStockphoto.
    com/Devonyu (p. 15); *Shutterstock*: Galyna Andrushko (p. 9), Colette3 (p. 21), Critterbiz (p. 7), Stanislav Duben
    (pp. 5, 7, 29), Daniel Hebert (p. 13), Matthew Jacques (p. 4), Linda Macpherson (p. 18), nialat (p. 11), max voran
    (p. 13), Christopher Wood (p. 4).

Library of Congress Cataloging-in-Publication Data

Murray, Julie, 1969-
  Snowy owls / Julie Murray.
      pages cm. -- (Arctic animals)
  Audience: 7-11.
  ISBN 978-1-61783-801-9
1. Snowy Owl--Juvenile literature. I. Title.
  QL696.S83S66 2014
  598.9'7--dc23
                        2012049647

Contents

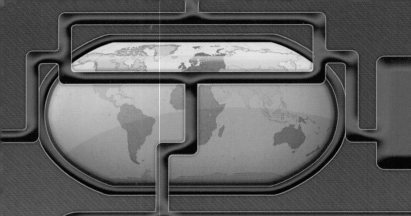

Earth has many different **regions**. But, few stand out as much as the Arctic. This is the northernmost part of Earth. The area is known for its freezing cold weather and great sheets of ice.

Snowy owls are known for their white feathers. These help them blend in with the Arctic's snowy land.

The Arctic includes land from several **continents**. It also includes the Arctic Ocean and the huge sea of ice that floats on it. The Arctic is home to many interesting animals. One of these is the snowy owl.

Snowy Owl Territory

Snowy owls live throughout the Arctic. This includes the northern parts of North America, Europe, and Asia.

Snowy owls live in the tundra. This large, flat part of the Arctic has very few trees. Some snowy owls **migrate** south during the winter. There, they live on farms, fields, **marshes**, or beaches.

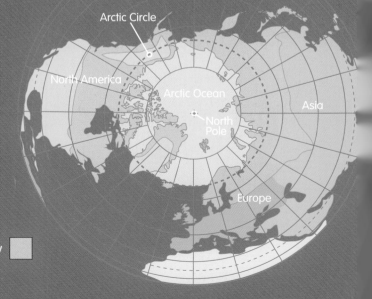

Arctic Circle

North America

Arctic Ocean

North Pole

Asia

Europe

Snowy Owl Territory

In the tundra, snowy owls sit on the ground. They look for hills, which allow them to see far. Farther south, they sit on fences, buildings, or posts.

Uncovered!
Snowy owls migrate if food becomes hard to find. They also migrate if the weather gets too cold or snowy.

Welcome to the Arctic!

If you took a trip to where snowy owls live, you might find...

...different countries.

Snowy owls live in many northern countries. These include the United States, Iceland, Russia, the United Kingdom, and Canada. Snowy owls are the official bird of the Canadian province of Quebec.

Gulf of Alaska

BEAUFORT SEA

Baffin Bay

GREENLAND
(Kalaallit
Nunaat

SEA

Denmark Strait

NORWEGIAN SEA

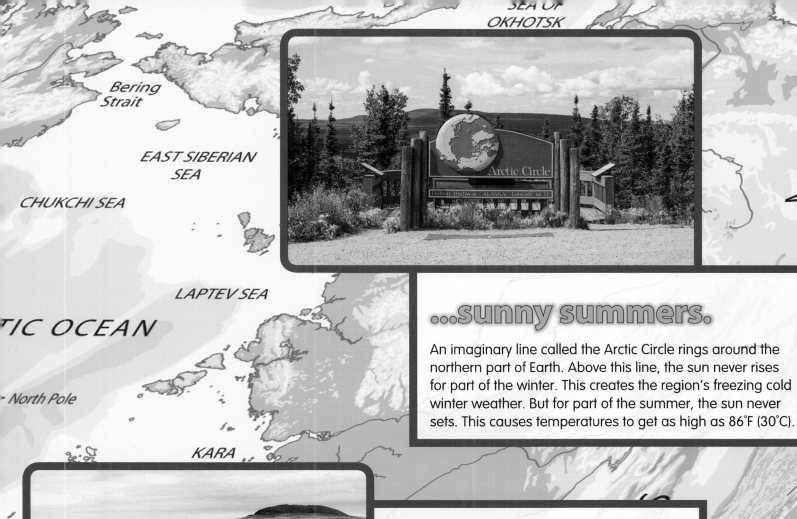

SEA OF OKHOTSK

Bering Strait

EAST SIBERIAN SEA

CHUKCHI SEA

LAPTEV SEA

...TIC OCEAN

North Pole

KARA

...sunny summers.

An imaginary line called the Arctic Circle rings around the northern part of Earth. Above this line, the sun never rises for part of the winter. This creates the region's freezing cold winter weather. But for part of the summer, the sun never sets. This causes temperatures to get as high as 86°F (30°C).

...permafrost.

Permafrost is land that stays frozen for at least two years. It is a main feature of the Arctic. In the southern Arctic, the top layer of permafrost melts during the summer. This allows plants to grow.

Take a Closer Look

Snowy owls have rounded bodies. They keep their thin legs and large wings tucked in when still.

A snowy owl's round head has small, yellow eyes and a small, dark bill. Unlike some owls, it does not have long tufts of feathers that look like ears.

A snowy owl's bill has a sharp point. It is very strong.

Snowy owls are large owls. Adults are 20 to 28 inches (51 to 71 cm) tall. Their wings are about 50 to 66 inches (127 to 168 cm) from tip to tip. Adult snowy owls weigh 1.5 to 6.5 pounds (0.7 to 3 kg). Females are usually larger than males.

A snowy owl has special feathers on its wings. These help an owl stay almost soundless while it flies.

Snowy owls are the heaviest owls in North America.

Feathered Fliers

Snowy owls are covered in thick feathers. Adult females are white with brown spots. Adult males are mostly white. Older males may be all white except for a few dark bars on their tails.

Uncovered!

A snowy owl's thick feathers help keep it warm in the Arctic. There, it can be as cold as -76°F (-60°C) during the winter!

Younger owls generally have more brown spots than older owls. All adults have white faces.

Mealtime

Snowy owls are **carnivores**. They mainly eat small **mammals** called lemmings. Sometimes, they eat mice, squirrels, rabbits, and hares. And, snowy owls eat bugs and fish. They also eat birds such as ptarmigan, ducks, and geese.

Uncovered!
After a snowy owl eats, it throws up parts of its prey that its body doesn't use. This includes the bones and fur.

Snowy owls don't chew their food. If their prey is small, they swallow it whole. If it is large, they use their claws and bills to tear it into small chunks before eating.

When enough lemmings are available, snowy owls will eat nothing else. An adult snowy owl eats three to five lemmings each day.

Great Hunters

Snowy owls are good hunters. They can catch **prey** on land, in the air, or from the surface of water.

Snowy owls hunt in sunlight and darkness. They hold still and wait to find prey. Snowy owls use their strong senses of sight and hearing to find prey. Then, they fly after it.

Snowy owls can turn their heads very far. This helps them spot prey.

Snowy owls use their sharp claws to grab prey.

Family Life

Snowy owls generally live alone. But, each spring they form pairs for mating. Males try to stand out by making fancy flights for females. Sometimes, they hold food in their claws or bills while flying.

During the mating season, each pair of snowy owls has its own home area. Pairs usually do not let others enter their home areas. They warn them to stay away by making noises.

If an owl has migrated south, it returns to the Arctic tundra to have babies.

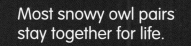
Most snowy owl pairs stay together for life.

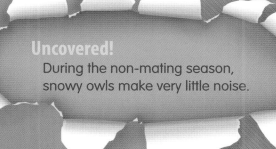
Uncovered!
During the non-mating season, snowy owls make very little noise.

Incredible Eggs

Before laying eggs, a female snowy owl makes a nest. She uses her claws to dig a shallow hole in the ground. She usually digs her nest on the top of a hill. This gives her a good view of her surroundings.

Sometimes, snowy owls use the same nest several years in a row.

A female snowy owl lays 3 to 11 eggs in her nest. The number of eggs depends on how much food is available. When there is not much food, snowy owls may not **mate** at all.

Snowy owl eggs are white. They are about two inches (5 cm) long. The mother owl sits on her eggs to keep them warm. Her mate guards the nest. After 31 to 34 days, the eggs **hatch**.

Uncovered!
Male snowy owls guard their nests closely. They even attack wolves that get too close!

A mother owl's mate brings her food while she sits on her eggs.

Baby Owls

Baby snowy owls are called chicks. Newly **hatched** chicks are blind and helpless. They stay in their nest with their mother. Their father brings them food.

Snowy owl chicks leave the nest after 14 to 26 days. But, they cannot fly and they still depend on their parents for care. After about seven to ten weeks, chicks are ready to live on their own.

Newly hatched snowy owls have soft, white feathers (*left*). Their feathers change as they grow (*below*).

Survivors

Life in the Arctic isn't easy for snowy owls. Some people hunt them for their meat and feathers. Snowy owls are **prey** for foxes, wolves, and coyotes. And, they risk running into power lines, cars, and airplanes.

Still, snowy owls **survive**. Their Arctic nesting grounds are largely not bothered by people. And, there are laws that limit hunting them. Snowy owls help make the Arctic an amazing place.

Snowy owls live about ten years in the wild.

Wow!
I'll bet you never knew...

...that snowy owls have many nicknames. These include Arctic owls, great white owls, ghost owls, tundra ghosts, Scandinavian nightbirds, and white terrors of the north.

...that Harry Potter's owl, Hedwig, was played by a male snowy owl. Even though Hedwig is a female character, male owls represented her in the movies. Males have whiter feathers. They are also smaller and easier to handle.

...that snowy owls often travel very far during their lifetimes. One snowy owl chick traveled from Victoria Island in Canada all the way to Russia!

Important Words

carnivore (KAHR-nuh-vawr) an animal or a plant that eats meat.

continent one of Earth's seven main land areas.

hatch to be born from an egg.

mammal a member of a group of living beings. Mammals make milk to feed their babies and usually have hair or fur on their skin.

marsh an area of low, wet land.

mate to join as a couple in order to reproduce, or have babies. A mate is a partner to join with in order to reproduce.

migrate to move from one place to another to find food or have babies.

prey an animal hunted or killed by a predator for food.

region a large part of the world that is different from other parts.

survive to continue to live or exist.

Web Sites

To learn more about snowy owls, visit ABDO Publishing Company online. Web sites about snowy owls are featured on our Book Links page. These links are routinely monitored and updated to provide the most current information available.

www.abdopublishing.com

Index